HAWAII The Big Island

Nene, or Hawaiian Goose, dawn.

CONTENTS

4 Discovering An Island

10 Celebrating The Land

19 A Window On Space

26 The Search For Alternate Energy

32 The Energy Of A People

38 An Island At Work

52 A Way Of Life To Share

72 Credits and Appreciations

Front cover: Student Daphne Wingate, Kealakehe School, May Day celebration. Photograph by Noel Black.
Back cover: Moon set over shadow of Mauna Kea from Mauna Kea with Hualalai in left middleground. Photograph by Carl A. Wilmington.

Printed in Singapore.

HAWAII The Big Island

A PRESS
PACIFICA
BOOK

Text/Gretel Blickhahn McLane
Editor/Robert B. Goodman
Associate Editor/Reginald E. David

Discovering An Island

THE BIG ISLAND of Hawaii is an exciting place to be. It is a land rich in its legacy and endowed with enormous potential. The chemistry of the island takes the fullness of its Hawaiian heritage, adds its many cultural strains and blends in ingenuity, ambition and modern science. The result? A place stirring with new projects and ideas.

Hawaii, the youngest of the Hawaiian Islands, is still pulsing with volcanic life. The sense of life and growth and change of the volcano is reflected in the energy of the island's people. The breadth of the scientific exploration being conducted on the Big Island is truly astonishing. In the field of art, painters, sculptors, writers, and dancers are

Previous page: Hawaiian voyaging canoe arriving during eruption of Mauna Loa.

not only delving into Hawaii's past, bringing to light neglected art forms, but are also building on these forms to break new ground, expanding the limits of creation by combining old forms and new techniques.

The Polynesians came to Hawaii in double-hulled voyaging canoes with a highly developed culture that had evolved in the South Pacific. Bringing with them the pig, chicken, and dog and about 24 varieties of plants, the people set up a system of agriculture based on a harmonious balance with Nature. Distribution of goods and services was accomplished by means of an intricate system of reciprocal gift-giving.

Government was organized according to an authority structure based on age and rank. Ruling chiefs received unquestioning obedience from those below them in the hierarchy. Kamehameha, Hawaii's most famous king of modern times, was born on the Big Island in the northern district of Kohala. Kamehameha was a shrewd trader and was able to make use of the white man and his weapons to conquer all the islands except Kauai, which was later ceded to his rule. He proved to be a wise and benevolent ruler, capable of handling the extraordinarily difficult task of bridging the widening gap between the new and old cultures. The last seven years of his life he reigned from Kona, dying there in 1819.

Chants and dances recorded the deeds and battles of great leaders like Kamehameha. The hula taught history, transmitted beliefs and customs, honored famous people, and extolled the virtues of industry and teamwork that were so important to everyone's survival.

The cultural renaissance of the Hawaiians, which has been growing over the past decade, recognizes and expands on the strengths of the ancient hulas, as well as creating some spectacular new dances, suitable for the modern age. The cultural revival is especially vibrant on the Big Island, where there is a well-defined Hawaiian population, and this revival adds a special dimension to living in this exceptional place.

Left: Nose flute player, 10th anniversary celebration, Pu'uhonua o Honaunau National Historical Park, South Kona.
Right: Hula dancer Brenda Alidon, Miss Aloha Hula 1981, dancing at the Pa Hula at Ka'auea.

Reminders of Hawaii's history exist all over the Big Island. Its districts remain those of long ago. The island is divided like a pie into six uneven wedges; counterclockwise, they are: Hilo, Hamakua, Kohala, Kona, Ka'u, and Puna. Kamehameha's first stronghold was the northern districts of Hamakua and Kohala, and he later made his capital on the western coast in Kona. Today the mayor and the county council carry on their business on the eastern coast, in the district and city of Hilo. Hilo is the largest city outside Oahu, and functions as the seat of government, the gateway to the rest of the island, and the commercial center of the county. Handsome contemporary state and county buildings are set off by a spacious park. Buying, selling, and banking chores of the island are carried on in an environment of wide lawns and plentiful flowers. Abundant rainfall keeps the city clean and green; Hilo is known for its nurseries and gardens. The city's Liliuoka-lani Gardens is a neat Japanese-style park of 30 acres not far from the city center. A long breakwater stretches like a crooked arm out into the bay, protecting the deep-water port where sugar and other products are loaded for transport to other islands and the Main-land; and the rich smell of molasses hangs in the air. Across the bay, Mauna Kea domi-nates the city. On this side of the island, the atmosphere is businesslike.

King Kamehameha talking to his son, Liholiho. The setting is Kailua-Kona during the last years of Kamehameha's reign.

Painting by Herb Kane, from the collection of the Hotel King Kamehameha, 6 x 10 feet, oil on canvas.

Heading north from Hilo are the ancient battlefields of Hamakua, now covered with green sugar cane. In the old days, a tiny train chugged up and down the coast, carrying sugar to the port in Hilo. In the old days, too, the narrow road from Hilo to Waimea doggedly followed the coast to the back of each valley and out again onto every promontory, making an eight-hour journey out of what is today a 75-minute drive. Set well back on the slopes, affording a view overlooking the fields and far out across the Pacific, the modern highway leads past Honokaa, where the first macadamia nuts were planted in 1881. Farther up the coast, at Waipio Valley, tourists admire the spectacular 2,000-foot cliffs from a lookout or take the Waipio Valley Shuttle to the floor. The Hawaiian

royalty who used to live in this "Valley of the Kings" have long since departed and only a few taro farmers make their living there today.

The northernmost district is Kohala, and its northern point is 'Upolu. On the eastern side, turning inland to skirt the impassable coast north of Waipio Valley, is the little community of Kapa'au and the original version of the statue of Kamehameha seen in front of the Judiciary Building in Honolulu. It was made by an American in 1880 in Italy, only to be lost at sea, duplicated for Honolulu, retrieved from the sea and put up in Kohala in honor of Kamehameha's birthplace in that district. The Mo'okini Heiau (a stonewalled enclosure that served as a temple), also in Kohala, is one of two temples built in the 13th century by the famous high priest, Pa'ao.

On the western slopes of South Kohala are found the cattle ranches one would expect in the West. The grass here is bent double, bowing before the wind, and a line of windbreaking ironwoods cuts a distinctive landmark across the pastel hills. Cactus was introduced to these rolling pastures many years ago. When it proved to be a pest, most of it was eradicated. At one time there was forest and once there were rivers carving their way to the sea. The ancient name for the region, Waimea, means reddish water. Today the town is called both Waimea and Kamuela. Kamuela is the official post office designation to avoid confusion with Waimea on Kauai.

In South Kohala the Pu'ukohola (Hill of the Whale) Heiau near Kawaihae was the scene of Kamehameha's accession to power over the entire island. A prophet predicted that Kamehameha would conquer all of the islands if he would build a new heiau and dedicate it to his war god, Ku'ka'ili-moku. Legend says that some of the water-smoothed boulders for the construction of the mortarless walls were transported hand-to-hand, bucket-brigade fashion, for 30 miles across the northern tip of the island from Pololu Valley on the Kohala Coast. It was at Pu'ukohola that Kamehameha's chief rival, Keoua, was killed and Kamehameha became ruler of the island. In the next 20 years the prophecy was fulfilled and Kamehameha came to control all the islands. Today the heiau is a preserved national historic site.

Kamehameha did most of his traveling by canoe because land travel was arduous, but today the Queen Ka'ahumanu Highway cuts smoothly across the lava flats. Driving from

Kawaihae to Kailua-Kona, it is easy to imagine that the shapes in the grass-tufted undulations of lava are the rivals of the fire goddess, Pele, whom she has covered with stone. Along the coast luxury hotels have risen on the same sites where the Hawaiian nobility liked to spend their summers. The resorts have often preserved and restored the petroglyphs, caves, fishponds, foot trails, and heiaus in this area. To the south, the mountains slope westward toward the ocean, bearing on their slopes coffee and macadamia nuts. In Kona, the sun rises late, and sunsets linger over the sea.

Often colored by the setting sun is Kailua-Kona's lava rock and coral Mokuaikaua Church, built between 1823 and 1837 and the state's first Christian place of worship. Farther south along the coast is historic Kealakekua Bay, where in 1778 Kamehameha watched the arrival of Captain Cook's ships and where he probably witnessed Cook's death the following year.

At Pu'uhonua o Honaunau National His-torical Park in South Kona, Hawaiians give cultural demonstrations in the old arts of making tapa (bark cloth), weaving lauhala baskets and mats, carving images, and feather-working. The park was a place of sanctuary for Hawaiians. It includes three heiaus and the grounds of the residence of ancient ruling chiefs.

The southern corner of the island is called Ka'u. Na'alehu, near the eastern coast is the southernmost town in the United States. Ka Lae, or South Point, is America's southernmost part – and possibly moving still further south, for this is the land of the living volcano. The most recent lava flow came down the flank of Mauna Loa and poured into the ocean in 1868, two and a half miles from the actual tip of the island. A major portion of the land reserved as the Hawaii Volcanoes National Park lies in the Ka'u district, and the district encompasses much of the caldera, or large summit crater, of each of the two active volcanoes, Mauna Loa and Kilauea.

The beautiful fire goddess, Pele, and her

volcano home were the source of inspiration for the Hawaiian people for hundreds of years. A majority of all hula and chant is tied to Pele and Kilauea in some way. Many hulas tell the story of Pele and her favorite little sister, Hi'iaka, who became the supreme patroness of hula.

The eastern part of the island below Hilo Bay is the district of Puna. Puna is nearly as large as the entire island of Oahu, although it is one of the smaller districts on the Big Island. In Puna, quiet country living contrasts with the literally bubbling energy of geothermal wells, native ohia-tree forests include wild orchids planted years ago from the air, and modern road-side signs give the names of ancient Hawaiian land divisions. Sugar cane, long the main focus of its agriculture, is scheduled to be phased out. Everyone is speculating on the new possibilities for the land and a new identity for the area.

In historical times, the area was a potent religious center. In the mid 13th century, a high priest named Pa'ao arrived in Puna from Ra'iatea near Tahiti. He and his religion had a great influence on the culture and history of the Hawaiian people, and it was he who had the Waha'ula Heiau built in Puna, the first heiau of its type in the islands. This heiau, profoundly important to Hawaiian culture, has been carefully restored.

Hawaii's past is preserved in myth and chant and dance, in fish hooks and bird bones and ancient hearth, in pictures carved on stone. For many years that past was covered over and over again by the bustle and bias of the present. Today on the Big Island, anthropologists and dancers, scientists and storytellers are once more revealing to all of us Hawaii's long hidden history.

Left: Petroglyph Cave at Holei Pali, Hawaii Volcanoes National Park.
Below: The painting, The Petroglyph Maker, at Anaehoomalu, the King's Trail angling in the background.

Painting by Herb Kane, from the collection of E. Marshall, M.D.

Celebrating The Land

THE CITY DWELLER, the surfer, the farmer, and the family in search of a simpler, cleaner way of life can all find a place on the Big Island. Some residents are newcomers who may have left cold climates to come to Hawaii to work or retire. Others are the descendants of people who came for generous or selfish purposes, or just drifted to Hawaii: entrepreneurs, missionaries, whalers, plantation workers, merchants, and adventurers.

The Big Island is larger than all the other Hawaiian Islands combined. Within its shores are found 11 of the world's 13 climates – all except the Saharan and the Arctic. It is an island of variety. Here is found the majestic grandeur of great mountains, often tipped with snow, rising above mysterious, moon-like, lava wastelands. Pristine fern forests are only a short drive from cool, windy highlands or black-, white-, and even green-sand beaches. Rugged cliffs, carved by waterfalls, complement sunny flatlands.

To the Hawaiians, this beautiful land was a part of a harmonious universe in which each component, each man or fish or rock, was an

Above: Hula dancer in ti leaf rain cape, Hulihee Palace, Kailua-Kona.

Right: Trade wind swells pounding coast, Puna area near Waha'ula Heiau.

integral part of a perfect whole. The Hawaiians had no trouble perceiving the infinite variety of the gods, or the shifting multitude of different faces each god could assume. The forces of Nature were personal, intimately known. (There were 200 names for the rain, but no general word for weather.)

Personalities emerged from the land as gods, and one of the most fascinating was the fire goddess, Pele. There are many versions of the legend of Pele's arrival on the Big Island, but in most versions, she travels from a distant homeland by canoe and arrives first at Niihau, where she tries to dig a pit deep enough to house herself and her brothers and sister. She travels to Kauai, to Oahu, and all along the chain of islands, trying to dig a pit in each island where she can receive the lover she met on Kauai. At last she finds a home at Halemaumau, the crater within the large caldera at the summit of Kilauea volcano where she remains to this day.

Five major volcanoes formed the island of Hawaii. The Kohala Mountains on the northern point are 5,000 feet tall and are classified as extinct. Hualalai, measuring 8,271 feet high, last erupted in 1801. Mauna Kea, the white mountain, is the tallest mountain in the world at 37,000 feet, if measured from the ocean floor to its summit, 13,796 feet above

sea level. It last erupted 3,600 years ago, and is considered dormant.

The two frequently active volcanoes are Mauna Loa (the long mountain) and Kilauea. Mauna Loa (13,677 feet high) is more than three times the height of Kilauea (4,000 feet high) and is the most massive mountain and the largest single land mass in the world. It measures six miles from the sea floor to its summit. Mauna Loa is the world's most prolific volcano, although Kilauea is the most active. They are both shield volcanoes, formed, layer upon layer, in the shape of gently curved shields.

Jack Lockwood, a geologist with the U.S. Geological Survey, says, "I'm the luckiest guy in the world to be at the Hawaii Volcanoes National Park, where the oldest rock around is only 1,500 years old. Most of what you see," he says, gesturing through the window of the Hawaiian Volcano Observatory at Kilauea, "was formed during Hawaii's recorded history – 200 years. Probably half the people on the island have physically seen this formed. Nowhere in the U.S. is the land so young."

Kilauea is Hawaii's "drive-in" volcano. Kilauea and Mauna Loa are probably the only volcanoes in the world where people rush toward them to see the eruption, rather than rush away to save themselves. On the scale of volcano violence, "Hawaiian" is the name given to the gentlest classification. Unlike the steam-spitting, ash-spewing, rock-exploding volcanoes around the Pacific "ring of fire," these volcanoes in the middle of the ocean are quite easy to get along with. Because the magma, or liquid rock, of Hawaiian volcanoes differs in chemical composition from the molten rock of, say, Mount St. Helens, it is less viscous, or resistant to flow. There is less water in Hawaiian magma, and it has a higher temperature. For all these reasons, steam and gas can bubble out of a Hawaiian volcano, releasing the pressure that builds to explosive proportions in less fortunate areas. Fortunately, too, the strong smell of any sulfur dioxide gas released by the volcano is its own warning.

Previous page: Young Koa trees and Tritonia grass, Hawaii Volcanoes National Park campground.
Above left: Kona Sunset.
Right: Waterfall above Pahala, Ka'u District.

A Window
On Space

THE POLYNESIAN NAVIGATORS were scholar-scientists of their time, observing, experimenting, reasoning and passing their knowledge on by teaching it to each succeeding generation.

One of the most exciting aspects of life on the Big Island today is the scope and importance of scientific research being carried on by present-day scholar-scientists, some of whom are examining the same stars that led the Polynesian canoes across the miles of open sea over a thousand years ago.

Today, scholar-scientists from around the world petition for time at the observatories on top of Mauna Kea. And what a magnificent site it is.

The island's distance from air pollution, the mountain's height, and the inversion layer of air that insulates its summit contribute to the clarity of the air at the top. At almost 14,000 feet, the air is thin, with much less visual distortion than is found at lower altitudes. Sixty percent of the nights on Mauna Kea are cloudless and permit perfect viewing.

There are six telescopes at Mauna Kea. The two small 24-inch telescopes, one sponsored by the University of Hawaii (UH) and the United States Air Force, and the other by the UH and the National Aeronautics and Space Administration (NASA), were installed in 1968 and 1969. In 1970 an optical/infrared 88-inch telescope, again sponsored by the UH and NASA, was the first of the four major telescopes to be placed on the site. In 1979, three more major telescopes joined the summit conference: a NASA infrared 120-inch telescope; a 144-inch optical/infrared 120-inch telescope; jointly sponsored by Canada,

Left: University of Hawaii 88-inch optical/infrared telescope at dawn.
Following spread: Volcanologist Jack Lockwood retrieves lava sample.

France, and Hawaii; and a giant 150-inch infrared telescope sponsored by the United Kingdom.

Eventually there may be as many as 13 telescopes on Mauna Kea. The University of California is working on a "next generation" model to create an ever-larger lens without becoming too weighty. This new design will put segmented mirrors in a circle to be integrated by means of computer control, and it will have an incredible effective aperture of 400 inches.

At South Point, a quite different project connected with space is in the negotiating stages. South Point is the site of ancient canoe moorings carved in stone, a reminder that canoes were formerly launched from these shores. Now, a Houston-based firm called Space Services, Inc. of America is interested in using the area to launch U.S. commercial satellites. Because firing could take place there on a path either along the equator or toward a polar orbit without endangering any land mass or populated area, South Point is unique as a possible satellite-launching location.

At present, all satellite launching is done by the federal government: by NASA or by

the military. What is being proposed is the launching by the private sector of much smaller, less costly vehicles, tailor-made with a specific business need in mind. Such satellites might be attractive to oil companies or to TV stations, telephone companies, or other large corporations with a need for the high-tech capability of instantaneous global communication. The company would like to see the first launch take place in 1984.

Jack Keppeler, former Big Island county managing director and consultant for the project, says, "It could lead to the far-out Buck Rogers ideas—like mining planets. Why not? The Big Island could be on the edge of a whole new space frontier." Keppeler sees the launch base as a mutually supporting addition to the numerous scientific facilities all over the Big Island.

One such facility, frequently overshadowed by the glamorous, star-gazing Mauna Kea Observatory, is located on the slopes of Mauna Loa and is called the Mauna Loa Observatory. What is being observed there is our own earth's atmosphere.

At an elevation of 11,150 feet, the Mauna Loa site has the same excellent observing conditions as Mauna Kea. In fact, Mauna Loa

conditions are slightly better for studying the earth's atmosphere because Mauna Kea's road sometimes causes dust, and Mauna Loa has the added advantage of being on the lee side of the taller mountain.

What started as a small weather station in the early 1950's was dedicated as the Mauna Loa Observatory (MLO) in 1956 by the U.S. Weather Bureau. Since 1971, it has been one of four observatories in the network of the National Oceanic and Atmospheric Administration (NOAA)'s Geophysical Monitoring for Climatic Change.

The MLO is low key, but its work is world renowned and is increasingly important as we become more concerned with environmental pollution. It is the only place in the world where continuous carbon-dioxide measurements have been made over the last two decades. Its studies of polluting particles, ozone, carbon monoxide, solar radiation, rainfall acidity, wind, and other weather measurements make a vital contribution to our understanding of how human activity affects the environment and vice versa. Scientists were subjected to search procedures on their way to the observatory.

The Mauna Loa Observatory has benefited from a relationship with another facility that one scientist called a "scientific gold mine." The MLO has had administrative offices from time to time on the University of Hawaii at Hilo campus next to the Cloud Physics Observatory. This facility operates under the statewide University of Hawaii Meterology Department. Its function is the study of the microphysics of tropical clouds, more easily understood by the layman as the study of why it rains. The research could have profound implications for weather modifications and cloud seeding, and this observatory, too, has hosted visiting scientists from many parts of the Mainland and the world.

Another Mauna Loa research facility, formerly called the High Altitude Observatory, has been renamed the Mauna Loa Solar Observatory. Here scientists study the sun's corona.

Down slope of the Kilauea caldera is the Hawaiian Volcano Observatory, a world-

Left: "Earth" scientists attending Fourth Conference in Natural Sciences, Hawaii Field Research Center, Hawaii Volcanoes National Park.
Above right: Demonstration project in tumble culture to raise *nori*, an edible red seaweed.
Lower right: Fresh water prawn farmer and research scientist David Barclay with newly harvested prawns, Hawi, Kohala.

23

reknowned center of volcano research. The dream of a geologist, Dr. Thomas A. Jaggar, it began in 1912 with funds from the Massachusetts Institute of Technology's Whitney Fund and a group of Hawaii businessmen. The U.S. Weather Bureau took it over in 1919, and since 1948 it has operated under the auspices of the U.S. Geological Survey.

Geologist Jack Lockwood credits the extraordinary record of safety at the volcanoes to the unique and symbiotic relationship between the U.S. Geological Survey observatory and the Hawaii Volcanoes National Park. No other parks have such a relationship, he said.

"We have been totally successful in predicting 130 percent of the eruptions," he said. "We have predicted a few that haven't come yet and have got the park rangers up in the middle of the night for nothing, but we haven't missed any."

The National Park Service is a scientific asset to the Big Island for its research and restoration of precious Hawaiian sites, for its support of the volcano observatory, and also for its research on native plants and animals, particularly endangered species. This research is carried out at the Hawaii Field Research Center (formerly the Mauna Loa Field Station), by the University of Hawaii, the U.S. Fish and Wildlife Service, and the National Park Service.

The park service is a primary agency sponsoring a biennial conference at the Volcano where "terrestrial" scientists (as opposed to "space" scientists or "marine" scientists) discuss research in natural sciences in Hawaii. The focus of the 1982 conference was the *nene*, the endangered Hawaiian goose.

Studies of less endangered species, such as papaya, macadamia nuts, vegetables, coffee, avocado, sugar cane, alfalfa, and guava are carried on all over the island at the Hawaii Agricultural Experiment Station. University of Hawaii faculty address everything from cultivating the soil to cultivating consumer interest, from fertilization and farm mechanization to family and community affairs, as well as developing novel varieties of both anthuriums and orchids.

On the federal level, support for the island agricultural industry comes from a little-known science facility with big national ramifications. It is a unit of the U.S. Agriculture Department's Hawaiian Fruit Flies Laboratory and is located on the 270-acre Waiakea Experimental Farm in Hilo.

The laboratory's development of safe fu-migation techniques opened the export market to the Hawaiian papaya. It is giving practical help to the island agricultural industry by researching new kinds of packaging and by working with fruit purees.

The raising of fish and plants in fish ponds has been part of Hawaii for over 600 years and is once more on the rise after a period of severe neglect. Successful and productive aquaculture studies are done at the Natural Energy Laboratory of Hawaii (NELH) in North Kona, home of the alternate-energy technology known as OTEC, or ocean thermal energy conversion. OTEC requires a flow of both warm surface ocean water and cold water from the ocean depths rich in the nutrients that plants love, and recent experiments have shown that the black seaweed called *nori* thrives in this water without any other nourishment.

Experimental colonies of salmon, trout and tilapia have done well at NELH. Jan War, operations manager of the laboratory, says they have improved the flavor of tilapia by gradually switching it from 100 percent fresh water to 100 percent salt water. Now tilapia, once shunned as a food fish because of its looks, is being hybridized to be more attractive to the marketplace.

Right: Dr. John Armstrong with laboratory raised adult oriental fruit flies to be used to infest fruits and vegetables for research.

Above: In the laboratory research process, fruit samples are impregnated with fruit flies to test the effects of various fumigation methods.

The Search For Alternate Energy

WHEN IT COMES to natural energy, the Big Island has a potential surplus, a big attraction for new industries. As a result, the Big Island is the site of an impressive variety of pilot projects in alternate energy sources.

The same North Kona NELH involved in aquaculture studies has been conducting research on ocean thermal energy conversion (OTEC) since 1975.

The Natural Energy Lab's 328-acres of sun heated lava flats at Ke-ahole Point is considered to be one of the best in the world for OTEC research and is the only one of five U.S. sites still being used. When all federal funding was cut off on October 1, 1981, the state stepped in. "We have a dedicated state and county government behind us," says NELH Operations Manager, Jan War.

The principle of OTEC, in the "closed-cycle" system, is to use the difference in temperatures between the warm surface water and the cold depths of the ocean to evaporate and condense alternately a fluid such as ammonia, which in turn activates a turbine and generator. Jan War explains the OTEC machine as a "giant refrigerator running in reverse."

On January 1, 1982, the first cold-water-to-shore pipe in the U.S. was put in place at NELH. It extends over a mile into the sea to a depth of 2,000 feet.

Experiments for several years have been concerned with biofouling (the accumulation of algae and other small sea life on heat exchangers), corrosion, and cleaning.

NELH floated the world's first pilot plant, dubbed Mini-OTEC, from August to November 1979. It was a 50-kilowatt version of proposed sea-based generating plants and operated from a former Navy scow. It was the first actual proof anywhere that a floating, closed-cycle OTEC plant could generate more electricity than it consumed.

A federal project, OTEC-1 operated off Ke-ahole Point in 1980-1981 for four months from the former Navy T-2 tanker, the Chepachet. Rechristened the SS Ocean Energy Converter, it tested heat exchangers capable of supporting a one-megawatt generator. Title to the ship has been transferred from the federal government to the state. NELH hopes to use the cold-water pipes from OTEC-1 to expand its cold-water capacity from the present 1,500 gallons per minute to 23,000 gallons per minute.

Above: Mini OTEC on station, off Ke-ahole Point, Kona.
Right: Biofouling research experiment and attending diver, NELH Operations Manager Jan War.

OTEC is not the only project which combines salt water and North Kona sunshine to form electricity. Ke-ahole Point will be the first site in the state to host a solar pond. Like OTEC, a solar pond uses two different water temperatures: warm water to vaporize a liquid which activates a turbine, and cold water to condense the liquid and complete the cycle. The temperature difference in a solar pond is created with two layers of water. A top layer of fresh water remains at air temperature – about 75°F. Like a one-way window, the top layer permits the sun's rays to penetrate, but prevents the heat from

leaving. In this way, heat is trapped in the bottom layer of dense salt water, and builds up to a temperature of about 200°F.

The state Department of Planning and Economic Development and Sets, Inc., a high technology firm of Honolulu, have initiated a contract for the design of an initial 30-kilowatt proof-of-concept pond and the conceptual design of a 300-kilowatt or larger pond.

If the 30-kilowatt demonstration pond is successful and if funding is then available, the next step will be to build a 20-acre solar-pond power plant. Power from the ponds will be used by the Kona Airport at Ke-ahole and by NELH.

The Big Island is also the location of the first home in the state to depend totally on sun power with no backup line to the electric company. The home has both a photo-voltaic-cell array to provide electricity, and solar panels for heating water.

The most promising of the new energy technologies is geothermal, which in Hawaii has made the leap from the experimental to the economically viable. Geothermal energy means that wells drilled into volcanically heated rock can be used to create steam to

Left: Testing 8,000 foot deep Puna geothermal well by measuring actual water and steam flow. Steam cloud, chemically scrubbed, is practically odorless.
Above: Three windmills, generating electricity, at ranch in Waimea.

power a conventional generator. With state funds, research was started in 1972; in 1975, drilling started on a small pilot-project well in Puna in connection with the Research Corporation of the University of Hawaii. After the well successfully opened in July 1976, the federal Department of Energy committed $10 million for a demonstration geothermal electrical-power plant. Hawaii is the second state in the union to have such a plant in operation.

Described by Hawaii Electric Light Co. (HELCO)'s project manager as a "hole in the ground with a bunch of valves," the 6,450-foot Hawaii Geothermal Project well and generator in Puna have been operating successfully since March 1982. The well is one of the hottest in the world at 358° C. Steam and hot water flow together to the surface, where they are separated, the water flowing off to a retaining pond, the precious steam channeled into a turbine.

Private companies are drilling test wells nearby and proposing the feasibility of expanding the production of geothermal energy. Under study is an undersea cable to carry excess energy to the other islands, particularly Oahu, 175 miles away. It is a challenging idea. The limits of present technology allowed an 1,800-foot deep, 78-mile long cable between Norway and Denmark. The 'Alenuihaha Channel between the Big Island and Maui is almost four times as deep, 6,900 feet.

Along the windward Hamakua Coast, where the sugar cane grows, the most productive of all the energy sources has gone beyond the developmental stage and is making a vital daily contribution. This is the burning of sugar-cane refuse, bagasse, which replaces much oil burning as a source of power for the sugar mills. Burning of bagasse provides almost 33 percent of the Big Island's electricity, saving the Big Island the cost of nearly 315,000 barrels of oil a year. The Davies-Hamakua plantation now uses a special patented process to pelletize the bagasse, making it both easier to store and usable on days when sugar is not being harvested.

With sugar acreage shrinking, HELCO will have to rely increasingly on burning some other biomass than bagasse. One such biomass alternative is "energy trees." C. Brewer & Co., through its BioEnergy Development Corporaion, is conducting a federally funded pilot project to explore the practicability of growing trees for fuel. Five hundred acres of fast-growing eucalyptus trees have been planted in Ka'u and along the Hamakua Coast. In five to seven years, the trees should reach a harvestable height of 50 to 60 feet, at which time they will be chipped and used as fuel at the sugar-plantation power plants. If the project is an economic success, C. Brewer plans to expand the operation and plant 3,000 to 4,000 acres of the trees along the Hamakua Coast.

While Puna is the home of geothermal electricity and Hamakua uses biomass, Kohala, to the north is lighting its houses with the wind. The Kahua Ranch, at an elevation of 3,250 feet on the slopes of the Kohala Mountains, is a pioneer in the come back of wind energy. In 1979, the Department of Energy funded an experimental 40-kilowatt Mehrkam wind turbine generator on the ranch property, then gave it to the ranch when the money ran out. Kahua Ranch also purchased a 17-kilowatt Jacobs machine. Power from these machines is used on the ranch. In addition, the ranch has an agreement with the Synectics Group, Inc. of Washington, D.C. to put up 10 to 20 medium-sized wind machines on the ranch to produce one megawatt of electricity for sale to HELCO. The ranch has made and is continuing to make a valuable contribution to wind research that can benefit the entire country.

Kahua Ranch Manager Monty Richards thinks that where windmills are concerned, small is beautiful. "If you build them too big, the numbers don't work out. Wind is only part of the answer to the energy needs. Some advantages are that they do not spoil the land and it is possible to 'double dip' and use the same land for both windmills and grazing. It's not even fenced," says Richards of one of his windmills. "The animals graze under it and rub against it. It doesn't bother them and they don't bother the windmill."

Right: World leaders in generating electricity from bagasse, three Big Island sugar companies save the equivalent of 315,000 barrels of imported oil per year. Generating plant smokestack vents steam derived from burning the bagasse.

The Energy Of A People

THE ISLAND OF HAWAII is a new land, still filled with the gift of energy. Its people have always expressed this energy in their enthusiasm for everyday living, especially in sports.

The ancient Hawaiian people reveled in their games and contests, particularly during the four-month "makahiki" season in the fall when war was outlawed. At that time, the people could cheer their favorites while the warriors continued to polish their skills with contests such as spear throwing, pole vaulting, wrestling, and boxing.

Today, on the Island of Hawaii there is a sport for everyone. For those who like to test themselves to the limit, there is the Original Ironman Triathlon World Championship. The grueling race consists of a 2.4-mile rough-water swim, followed by a 112-mile bicycle race and a 26.2-mile marathon. In spite of its name, the Ironman Triathlon is open to both men and women. It is held annually in Kona in October.

On top of Mauna Kea, there is even snow for skiers. It is usually possible to ski on Mauna Kea at an elevation of 13,680 and higher, from the beginning of the year until

An Island
At Work

THE FIRST POLYNESIAN settlers brought with them the plants and animals they needed to sustain their lives and their beliefs. Pigs and dogs and chickens, as well as coconut palms and banana plants and breadfruit shoots, were tended carefully on board the canoes, and when drinking water became scarce during the voyages, the animals and plants were given a ration before the men and women.

Once landed, these living things were nurtured with reverence. They flourished, and, in return, the settlers flourished and multiplied. In 1778, James King, a young lieutenant with Captain Cook, estimated that there were 10,000 people at Kealakekua Bay watching the ships' arrival.

After the island's "discovery" by white men, the number of different plants and animals in the islands increased rapidly. In 1793, on another British ship, Captain George Vancouver, brought the first cattle to Kamehameha at Kealakekua Bay. The animals were given the protection of a 10-year kapu, or taboo, during which time they were allowed to roam freely and not molested in any way. They multiplied into herds of thou-

Above: Paniolo, Parker Ranch, Waimea.
Right: Annual Parker Ranch Bull and Horse Sale, Waimea.

revival of interest in things Hawaiian. The Petroglyph Press gets its name from the Hawaiians' graphic communication through their stone carvings of shapes and figures. The Press was begun over twenty years ago. It publishes only Hawaiiana, and has over 30 titles in print.

The Volcano Art Center is housed in a former Volcano House hotel located near the rim of the Kilauea caldera. It was built in 1877, post-and-beam style like a New Hampshire barn. When photographer Boone Morrison first saw it, it was boarded up and falling down, a place only an artist could love. With some government money and a lot of labor, the Morrisons restored the building and opened it in 1974 as the Volcano Art Center, now completely self-supporting through memberships and gallery sales.

The VAC provides a base for concerts, lectures, exhibits, and classes in every facet of art. Artists come from everywhere to participate in its retreats, artist-in-residence

Far left: University of Hawaii at Hilo sophomore, Lori Tanimoto.
Center: Campus Center, University of Hawaii at Hilo.
Above: Hawaii Preparatory Academy student, Stacy Little, explores English grammar on school's elaborate DEC computer system.

programs, Elderhostel seminars, and dance workshops, such as the major dance offering in the Pacific, the annual week-long Volcano Dance Retreat. The VAC functions as a communication center for the growing Volcano village community of local and visiting writers and artists it has been instrumental in creating. VAC Director Marsha Morrison draws a parallel between the energy of New York City and the "incredible magnetism" of the Volcano. She points out that as opposed to New York City, artists at the Volcano can find both the stimulation of other creative people as well as the unspoiled natural beauty they need to inspire their work. She continues, "Some of the finest art in the country is here. A chapter in the history of American art can be written from this island. . . . When we first opened, the walls were empty. Because we bothered to have a gallery, people are creating."

Below: Artist-historian Herb Kane in his Keauhou Beach Hotel studio.

Right: Boone and Marsha Morrison, Volcano Art Center.

Far right: Gourds for sale, hoolaulea, old Kona Airport.

A Way Of Life To Share

FOR CENTURIES THE Hawaiian religion directed the every day patterns of life. In the last century, under the tremendous influx of new religions and new cultures, much of the Hawaiian culture appeared to be lost.

The great King Kamehameha's death in 1819 left the kingdom in the hands of his favorite wife Ka'ahumanu, and his 22 year old heir, Liholiho. Ka'ahumanu made an ally of the late king's most sacred wife, Liholiho's mother, Keopuolani, and began to urge the young king to abandon the system of kapus or taboos that formed the basis of the Hawaiian religion and social structure. Only six months after Kamehameha's death, Liholiho took the irrevocable step of eating among the women at a feast at the Kamakahonu Beach in Kailua-Kona. He then ordered all heiaus and their images destroyed.

The first Protestant missionaries arrived at the same Kamakahonu Beach the following year, delighted to find that the religious coast was clear and convinced that their God had paved the way for them. By 1854, the American Board of Commissioners for Foreign Missions, which had sent the missionaries,

Above: Mokuaikaua Church and Hulihee Palace from Kailua Pier, evening.
Right: Children at play, oceanside, Kailua-Kona.

considered Hawaii to be a Christian nation.

Other religions and sects followed. The French brought Catholicism in 1827. They were followed by Irish and Belgian priests, most notably the famous Father Damien, who worked in Puna for several months and in Kohala/Hamakua for eight years before volunteering to go to Molokai's leper colony in 1873. The arrival of the Portuguese and Filipino laborers strengthened the Catholic Church. Interesting and beautiful churches were built, such as St. Benedict's Painted Church in South Kona and the painted Star of the Sea Church at Kalapana. Catholicism began its sponsorship of schools for children of every age.

Germans brought the Lutheran religion to the islands, and during the last century the Mormons, Methodists, and the Salvation Army all arrived. The Chinese laborers who came between 1852 and 1876 (for $3 a month) brought with them a religion which was a blend of Taoism, Buddhism, and Confucianism. On the plantations, Japanese ministers from San Francisco tried, not too successfully, to convert to Christianity the many Japanese laborers who had brought the five major sects of Buddhism with them to the islands. The first Buddhist worship hall of any kind in Hawaii was built in Hilo. It was a tiny place, only 20 by 30 feet, with a high, sloping roof and traditional upturned corners to deflect demons.

In the 20th century, Greek Orthodox services were held for many years under the leadership of "Uncle George" Lycurgus of the Volcano House. Others who arrived more recently were the Baptists, Unitarians, Presbyterians, Quakers, and Jews.

The cross-pollination of all these different customs and religions gives rise to some interesting effects in modern Hawaii. Devout Catholics, Protestants, and Buddhists throw ohelo berries or gin into Halemaumau for the goddess Pele. Hawaiian Christian ministers bless occasions, buildings, and babies with the ancient symbols of salt water and ti leaves. Modern brides make the traditional Japanese gold cranes for good luck, and wear something borrowed, something blue down

Left: People, Magic Sands Beach, Kailua-Kona.
Right: Bride and friend, Hawaiian wedding celebration by the sea, Kailua-Kona.

the aisle. After the wedding, the luau can start with champagne and *sashimi* (raw fish), followed by authentic poi and ground-oven-cooked pork supplemented with *sushi* (rice cakes), potato salad, and soda pop. Elsewhere, at a Hawaiian bar mitzvah, the speaker admits he had to work to get his kippah (skullcap) to match his lei.

In the last century, traders like Richard Cleveland, who brought the first horses to the island, took three weeks to sail from California across the Pacific to Hawaii. Modern air transportation makes it in five hours today, less time than it takes to go coast to coast. Once you get to Hawaii, some reorientation is necessary. For example, the Far East is now due west; the Wild West is off to the northeast.

Behind the sometimes exotic facade of the island exists a supporting community of bankers, teachers, government workers, farmers, sales-people, and many others who contribute to the functioning of a modern community. Shopping on the Big Island can mean poking into tiny, family-owned shops or choosing from the large inventory of a modern department store. The covered, air-conditioned Kaiko'o Mall in Hilo is comparable to shopping centers anywhere in America. Stores such as Sure Save and KTA Super Stores use up-to-date computer technology to offer a complete selection of both Mainland products and Hawaii's own unique foods.

The state government has been said to have "the most openly accessible, the most comprehensible or least complex legislative system in the nation." (*The Sometime Governments, 1971.*) Below the state level are the four counties, neatly divided by islands. The Big Island is County of Hawaii, and is run by a mayor and county council of nine at-large members, all elected for four-year terms. A prosecuting attorney is the only other elected county official and is elected to a four-year term. Hilo is the county seat. There are no separate city governments with conflicting jurisdictions, and no overlapping districts such as transit, water, or school (except for the soil-conservation districts), which exist in other states.

The island has a beautiful international airport in Hilo, with direct flights to the mainland by United Airlines. There is also an airport in Kona at Ke-ahole Point, and smaller airports at Waimea and 'Upolu Point. Hilo Bay and Kawaihae Bay are deep-water ports.

The way of life on the Big Island includes live theater, and theater on the Big Island means one of two places. One is the facility of the University of Hawaii at Hilo, which is used for the UHH Vulcan Jazz Ensemble and the UHH Repertory Singers performances, as well as performances by the Honolulu Symphony, the Hilo Community Theater, the Hawaii Concert Society, the Lyceum Series, and other productions on tour from Honolulu and beyond.

The other choice is the newer 490-seat

Below: Hawaiian child and drum, tenth anniversary celebration for Pu'uhonua o Honaunau National Historical Park, Honaunau.
Right: Young Japanese dancer from Parker-Hirai Dance Studio, Hilo, performing at New Year's mochi ceremony, Volcano Art Center, Hawaii Volcanoes National Park.

Kahilu Theatre in Waimea, opened in 1981 by Parker Ranch owner, Richard Smart, himself a performer. The theater has brought a wide range of productions to Waimea, from musicals and drama to the Oakland ballet and kabuki.

When it comes to holidays, Hawaii gets them all. In addition to the standard Thanksgiving, Christmas, Easter, and so forth, there are dolls for Girls' Day and flying paper fish for Boys' Day. Ceremonies are held for Bodhi Day and during the summer, there is the O-Bon season, when Buddhist family and ancestors are honored with temple services and Bon dances.

Islanders recognize Malasadas Day and attend the Miss Hawaii Filipina Beauty Pageant, the Miss Hawaii Puerto Rican Beauty Pageant, and Miss America preliminary pageants. Celebrations are held on Prince Kuhio Day and Kamehameha Day, as well as May Day (Lei Day) and Aloha Week. Fireworks

explode on New Year's Eve and Chinese New Year's, in addition to the Fourth of July. The Kona Coffee Festival in the fall and the Miss Macadamia Nut Festival in August celebrate Big Island agricultural products.

One of the most important celebrations in

Above: "King's Kids" in the annual Kamehameha Day Parade, Kailua-Kona.
Right (upper and lower): Post Kamehameha Day Parade fun and games, old Kona Airport, Kailua-Kona.

Left: State office building, Hilo.
Below: Revived store, Kea'au.
Right: Star of the Sea Church, painted church, Kalapana.

Hawaii takes place on the Big Island and nowhere else. "If you want to see Hawaii, come see the Merrie Monarch Festival," says Dottie Thompson, the festival's chairman. The festival honors King Kalakaua, king of Hawaii from 1883 to 1891, one who loved a good party and who patronized a revival of the hula and other Hawaiian art. The annual festival, held in Hilo, originated in 1963 and now lasts for a week every April. There are lovely displays of Hawaiian handicrafts as well as demonstrations of haku lei making and lauhala weaving. But the *piece de resistance* is the statewide hula contest – performed to perfection including a Miss Aloha Hula contest for solo women dancers, and contests between the hula schools in both ancient and modern dance.

Another event unique to the Big Island, which draws huge crowds, this time inter-

national ones, is the prestigious five-day Hawaiian International Billfish Tournament. This has been a part of every Kailua-Kona summer since 1959. An average of 75 teams from all over the world compete to land the biggest "Pacific Blue" on no more than an 80-pound test line and take home a koa-wood trophy. Kona also holds a number of jackpot fishing tournaments throughout the year.

Tournaments aside, Big Island fishing is outstanding anytime. In June 1982, the world record for marlin caught on a rod and reel was set in Kailua-Kona with the catch of a 16-foot, 1,376-pound Pacific Blue Marlin by Jay deBeaubien of San Rafael, California. Charter boats are always available, and catches also include yellowfin tuna, mahimahi and bonito. Surf casting at South Point and freshwater fishing in the Waiakea Pond in Hilo are also popular pastimes.

Lindsey Pollock, senior vice president of Hawaiian Airlines, says the Big Island "has the most varied outdoor life of any island, whether you are talking about organized sports like tennis or golf, or the great outdoors, meaning hiking, swimming, fishing, hunting. For golf, there are some of the best courses in the world, and all close by and available all year long." The Big Island has eight full-size golf courses and two 9-hole courses. The Francis H. I'i Brown Golf Course at the Mauna Lani Resort has been called "one of the world's finest." It was also one of the nation's most expensive to build. The surf splashes up between the tee and fairway of the sixth hole. A former *Honolulu Advertiser* sports editor has suggested that the course is a collector's item. "If they ever put a golf course in the Smithsonian, this will be it."

Hiking and camping and family day trips are especially fine on the Big Island because of the island's diversity and the fact that everything is available within a relatively short radius. As Lindsey Pollock says, the feeling is that "the whole island is your back yard. There are many little villages bypassed

Left: The city of Hilo, Mauna Kea in the background.
Above: Merrie Monarch Hula Festival, Hilo Civic Auditorium.

by time and by highways. You can go back 50 years by driving 50 miles." In some areas, five miles will do it. Some of the coastal villages are the descendants of long-ago Hawaiian fishing villages, while others, picturesque and board-fronted, originated as plantation camps.

Nowhere in the islands does the cultural renaissance of the Hawaiians have more fertile ground than on the Big Island. Many Hawaiians serve as living resources to preserve their culture, and evidence of their religion and history is plentiful and accessible in the form of preserved historical sites all over the island. Visitors may see several heiaus, the rock-walled enclosures that served as temples, in various stages of restoration or simply protection. Pu'uhonua o Honaunau on the Kona Coast, was a special place of sanctuary for people accused of crimes or fleeing war. This sacred place was declared a National Historical Park in 1961 and has been beautifully restored. To the north in Kohala, the state has restored the ancient fishing village of Lapakahi so that people today can get a glimpse of life in Hawaii as it was in the 14th century. The 20-acre Kalani Honua "arts and agriculture farm" in Puna looks like a resort, but teaches about the arts and Hawaiian language and culture, with a lot of help from the surrounding community.

Modern resorts are conscious about keeping the integrity of the land they build on and of restoring and preserving the land's cultural treasures. Most of these resorts and historic sites are found along the Kona Coast. Artist Herb Kane says there is more of old Hawaii in Kona than anywhere else in the islands. There are 35 historic sites just on the slope behind the Keauhou Beach Hotel, where Kane is artist-in-residence. At this hotel it is possible to see huge stone fishing shrines (brought from Maui 400 years ago), King Kalakaua's fishpond (stocked with fish and turtles), Kalakaua's beach house (two bedrooms and no kitchen), the Kapuanoni Heiau in front of the hotel (used for rest and recreation and summit meetings by royalty), the Hapai Ali'i Heiau (for prayer and possibly birthing), and the Ke'eku Heiau (where the king of Maui invaded 400 years ago and was defeated and sacrificed).

Left: Pacific marlin leaps to break free of hook in lower jaw during Kona fishing tournament.
Below: Kailua-Kona and Kailua Bay.

Across the Kahalu'u Beach Park can be seen the Kuemanu Heiau. This was a surfing heiau, since the nobility had to leave the shore from consecrated land.

Up the coast in Kailua-Kona, next to the Hotel King Kamehameha, is the Ahu'ena Heiau, where King Kamehameha died, where the eating kapu was broken by Liholiho, where he heard lectures each evening to prepare him for the monarchy.

Farther north, the Kona Village Resort, the Waikoloa Resort at 'Anaeho'omalu Bay, and the Mauna Lani Resort have restored ancient royal fishponds and preserved petroglyphs. Portions of the king's trail, a pathway of lava used by runners, can be seen at Waikoloa and Mauna Lani.

To Guido Giacometti, president of the Bishop Estate's Kamehameha Investment Corporation, a hotel and resort is the beginning of permanent residence. "The golf club (in Keauhou) is filled now with people who own a condo in Kona. They live in Washington or California or some other state, and after a few years of doing this, they turn into residents of Hawaii." These residents buy land and houses, pay taxes, and may even go into business.

Below left: Tourists watch pig being removed from imu for luau, Keauhou Beach Hotel, Keauhou.
Left: Salt water swimming pool, Kona Surf Hotel, Keauhou.
Below: Reconstructed 'Ahu'ena Heiau, Kamehameha's last temple dedicated to Lono, the god of peace and prosperity, Hotel King Kamehameha, Kailua-Kona. Dusk.

Giacometti says that on the west coast of Hawaii there is definite control of the amount of growth that will occur. Planning and zoning, as shown on the General Plan map, will maintain centers of growth, rather than a continuous strip. The Mauna Kea Beach Hotel and the Mauna Lani and Waikoloa resorts form a center to the north; to the south, there is only the reclusive Kona Village Resort for several miles along the coast. The strip of development from Kailua-Kona to Keauhou-Kona is the most concentrated, then there is nothing in the way of resorts all the way to South Point. Giacometti says: "Efforts will be made to change (the General Plan), but it will come hard." There is in the area a large amount of state land that will remain as open space.

There are excellent hotels and meeting

Right: Windsurfing off the beach at ʻAnaehoʻomalu.
Far right: Beach at ʻAnaehoʻomalu Bay fronting Sheraton Royal Waikoloa Hotel.
Below: Teeing off, sixth hole, Francis H. Iʻi Brown golf course, Mauna Lani Resort.

Right: Food preparation, the gourmet Tiare Room, Sheraton Royal Waikoloa Hotel, Waikoloa.
Below and right: Evening on the beach, couple and family, Waikoloa.

facilities on the eastern side of the island as well. Tourists enjoy Hilo's lush gardens, scenic waterfalls, and Lyman Mission House and Museum.

Hawaii is the leading state in the nation for life expectancy at birth for males and females combined (75.9 years, as opposed to 72.5 on the Mainland). Maybe, on the Big Island, that is because people on all sides think it is a happy place to live.

Mark Twain, writing from Kailua-Kona in the summer of 1866, said: "Ye weary ones that are sick of the labor and care, and the bewildering turmoil of the great world, . . . pack up your carpet sacks and go to Kailua! A week there ought to cure the saddest of you all." Many people have since taken his advice. Kailua-Kona has been fortunate for those who have found a home here: artists, travel industry persons, business entrepreneurs, professional men and women, and retirees. They have come from around the world, creating a sophisticated life style in a relaxed Hawaiian environment.

On the other side of the island, the University's Chancellor Mitchell speaks of the friendliness of Hilo: "This is a warm and gracious place. Here you can pick your own place and lifestyle. I find it hard to fit in everything I want to do." Bernard Nogues at Hawaii Preparatory Academy in Waimea says: "Here it is nice, safe, clean, not industrialized. People want to live here." And in the south, Marsha Morrison of the Volcano Art Center talks of the inspiration and magnetism to be found at the Volcano, and geologist Jack Lockwood thinks being on Hawaii makes him "the luckiest guy in the world."

This is the Big Island: beautiful, energetic, original, spacious enough to stretch in, small enough to feel like home, interesting enough for both oldtimers and newcomers, friendly enough for anyone.

CONTRIBUTORS

NOEL BLACK grew up in Hawaii and moved to the Big Island where she set up a commercial photography studio. Active in outrigger canoe paddling and other sporting activities, she collaborates and cohabitates with her husband, A.D. Ackerman who creates commercial video productions. Noel's work has been widely published in the U.S. and abroad. She can be reached at P.O. Box 715, Kealakekua, Hawaii 96750, phone (808) 322-3672.

JOE CARINI is a photographer deeply tuned to Hawaiians and the culture. Trained in still-photography at the University of Milwaukee, Crini first worked with David Cornwell, then expanded into film and video work with Hawaii's leading film producer. Editorial still-photography, however, remains his basic love. He can be reached at Bear Productions, 3543 Nuuanu Pali Drive, Honolulu, Hawaii 96817, phone (808) 595-2807.

DAVID CORNWELL lives and works in a Honolulu studio that is itself a flashback to late nineteenth century America. Cornwell's photography has been published everywhere and ranges from photo-journalism to the world of industry, or fashion. His company is David Cornwell Productions, Inc., 1311 Kalakaua Avenue, Honolulu, Hawaii, 96826, phone (808) 949-7000.

REGINALD "REGGIE" DAVID came to Hawaii eleven years ago after extensive travels in South America, the Middle East, and Europe. With his wife, Susan, he established the first professional lab on the Big Island to support his own freelance photography for clients like National Geographic, Anheuser Busch, United Airlines, Xerox, and many others. One of America's finest bird photographer teams, the Davids' make their home in Kailua-Kona and can be reached at Rana Productions, P.O. Box 1371, Kailua-Kona 96740, phone (808) 329-1245.

ROBERT B. GOODMAN came to Hawaii in 1959 to make his home. Working as a freelance photo-journalist, pictures he took of the Kilauea Iki eruption got him a staff position as a National Geographic photographer. Three years later he went on to fund and produce two best sellers, The Australians, and The Hawaiians. Goodman founded Island Heritage Publishing Company and with his partner, Robert Spicer created or published some eighty titles. Selling Island Heritage in 1979, Goodman and Spicer were invited by the Mexican government to create a special educational program now in more than 5,000 U.S. schools.

HERB KAWAINUI KANE (artist) was raised on the Big Island. Later, moving to the mainland, he established himself as one of America's top commercial illustrators. Kane returned to Hawaii in 1971, and together with friends and associates gave birth to the Polynesian Voyaging Society and the recreation of "Hokulea", an ocean going Polynesian voyaging canoe which was to successfully sail without instruments the ancient Polynesian star paths to Tahiti and back. Kane produced on assignment three major articles for National Geographic including a cultural map of Polynesia. His book, Voyage, The Discovery of Hawaii, has long been a best seller. Today, Herb Kane has his studio in the historically rich Keauhou Beach Hotel in Keauhou-Kona where he is working as an artist-historian recreating significant moments of Hawaii's past.

GRETEL B. McLANE (writer) was born in Deadwood, South Dakota and came to the Big Island at the age of eight when her father became editor of the Hilo Tribune Herald. A graduate of Hilo High School, Gretel went on to Stanford and later a Masters degree in French from San Francisco State University with studies both in the U.S. and France. The author of an outstanding new historical novel on Hawaii for children of all ages as well as numerous articles, Gretel has made her home in Honolulu since 1965 where she lives with her lawyer husband and two children, Keith and Katie. Correspondence will reach her care of the publisher.

BOONE MORRISON, a Big Island resident for more than ten years, specializes in creative photography. An architectural designer, musician and composer, graphic and museum designer, and of late, television director, he maintains his home and studios at Volcano Village. His photography is in private and institutional collections worldwide including New York's Museum of Modern Art. Boone can be contacted at P.O.Box 131, Volcano, Hawaii, 96785, phone (808) 967-7512.

CHRIS NEWBERT has been a Kona resident for twelve years. World famous as an award winning underwater photographer, Newbert has been published in National Geographic, Audubon, Oceans, and many other magazines. He presently is at work on two books, one on Australia's Coral Sea, and the second, a portfolio-book of his finest underwater photographs. Correspondence will reach him at P.O. Box 1953, Kailua-Kona Hawaii 96740, phone (808) 325-5589.

FRANK SALMOIRAGHI first came to Hawaii in 1968. He moved to the Big Island where he photographs professionally, teaches at the University, and gives numerous workshops. Salmoiraghi's photography has been collected and exhibited by major art galleries and institutions as well as featured in Orientations, the Swiss magazine Camera, and other publications. He is widely considered by his peers as a major photographic talent. He can be contacted at P.O. Box 120, Hilo, Hawaii 96720, phone (808) 959-3147.

EDITORIAL ADVISOR: Toni Yardley

CREDITS

Noel Black: Pages Front Cover, 10, 18-19, 29, 36 (lower), 52, 71 Tom Brown: Page 61 Joe Carini: 34, 63, Back Cover David Cornwell: Pages 10-11, 70 (lower) "Reggie" David: Pages 4, 12-13, 26, 32-33, 35 (upper), 37, 38-39, 52-53, 54, 55, 56, 59 (upper), 65, 68 (lower) Robert B. Goodman: Pages 22, 23, 24, 25, 28, 31, 36 (upper), 38, 40, 41, 42, 43, 45, 46, 47, 48, 49, 50, 51, 58, 59 (lower), 60 Herb Kane: (paintings) Pages 2-3, 6-7, 9 Boone Morrison: Pages 1, 5, 8, 20-21, 32, 44, 57 Chris Newbert: Pages 14, 35 (lower) Frank Salmoiraghi: Pages 15, 17 Betsey Zimmerman: Page 64 Hawaii Volcano Observatory: Page 16 Amfac Hotels: Pages 66, 67 (lower) InterIsland Resorts: Page 66 (upper) NELH: Page 27 County of Hawaii: Pages 62-63 Mauna Lani Resort: Page 68 (lower) Sheraton Hotels of the Pacific, Mike Horikawa: Pages 69, 70 (upper).

APPRECIATIONS

A.D. Ackerman, Chad Andagan, Captain Beans, Bruce Benson, "Bick" Bickson, Noel Black, Phyllis Branco, Ernest Bouvet, Dudley Child, Han Ching, Bob Cotter, K.L. Coulson, Thomas B. Crabb, Roy T. Cunningham, Keikilani Curnan, Reggie and Susan David, Ann Davison, John DeFries, Terrence Duarte, Annette Ebinger, Jon Erickson, Mr. and Mrs. Harry Fellerman, Brian and Sheryl Fellerman, Charles M. Fullerton, Charles Garcia, Jules and Soontaree Gervais, Guido L. Giacometti, Chuck Gibb, Susanne and Leonard Gines, Dan Gleason, Milton Goto, Masao Hanaoka, Alexa Holt, Slim Holt, Marvin Iida, Herb Kane, Mike Kaneda, William S. Kawahara, The Staff at the Keauhou Beach Hotel, Noel P. Kefford, Jack Keppeler, H. Stuart Kearns, Jr., William A. Koepke, Megumi Kon, Alvin Koo, Bob Krauss, Betty Krauss, Thomas A.Kreiger, Matalie Kosanoich, Rodney T. Lau, John P. Lockwood, Bob MacGregor, Nawelo Marciel, Charles McCrary, Douglas R. McLane, Kepa Maly, Mayor Herbert T. Matayoshi, Mary Matayoshi, Stephen R. Mitchell, Boone Morrison, Marsha Morrison, Bernard B. Nogues, Reggie Okamura, Norman A. Oss, Anna Lindsey Perry-Fiske, Lindsey N. Pollock, Meleanna Pricher, Richard and Jane Pultz, Rene Racine, The Staff at the Ranchouse, Stan Randolph, David K. Reed, Monty Richards, Ralph and Harriete Salee, Rick Scudder, Jerry Seely, Jan Selland, Valerie Silk, Sanderson Sims, Joseph K. Spencer III, Charles P. Stone, Jack K. Suwa, Ed Swofford, Howard A. Takata, Dick Tillson, Bert Thomas, Allyson Uratani, Bill Van Vechten, Douglas Victorino, Jan C. War, Yoshio Watanabe, Alan and Steve Wilcox, Leroy Williamson, Jim Woessner, Jeanne Yagi, Toni Yardley, Kim Zitter.

TYPESETTER: Stats 'n Graphics, 331-A Kamani Street, Honolulu, Hawaii 96813, (808) 538-1626 PRINTER: Tien Wah Press, Ltd., 977 Bukit Timah Road, Singapore 2158 DISTRIBUTOR: Pacific Trade Group, P.O. Box 1227, Kailua, Hawaii 96734, (808) 671-6735.

McLane, Gretel Blickhahn.
  Hawaii, the big island.

  1. Hawaii–Description and travel–1981-
I. Goodman, Robert B., editor. II. Title.
DU523.25.M34 1982   996.9'1   83-4418
ISBN 0-916630-35-8
ISBN 0-916630-34-X (pbk.)